MYSTERIOUS PYRAMIDS

Tikal:
Pyramids of the Ancient Maya

Murray "Oak" Tapeta

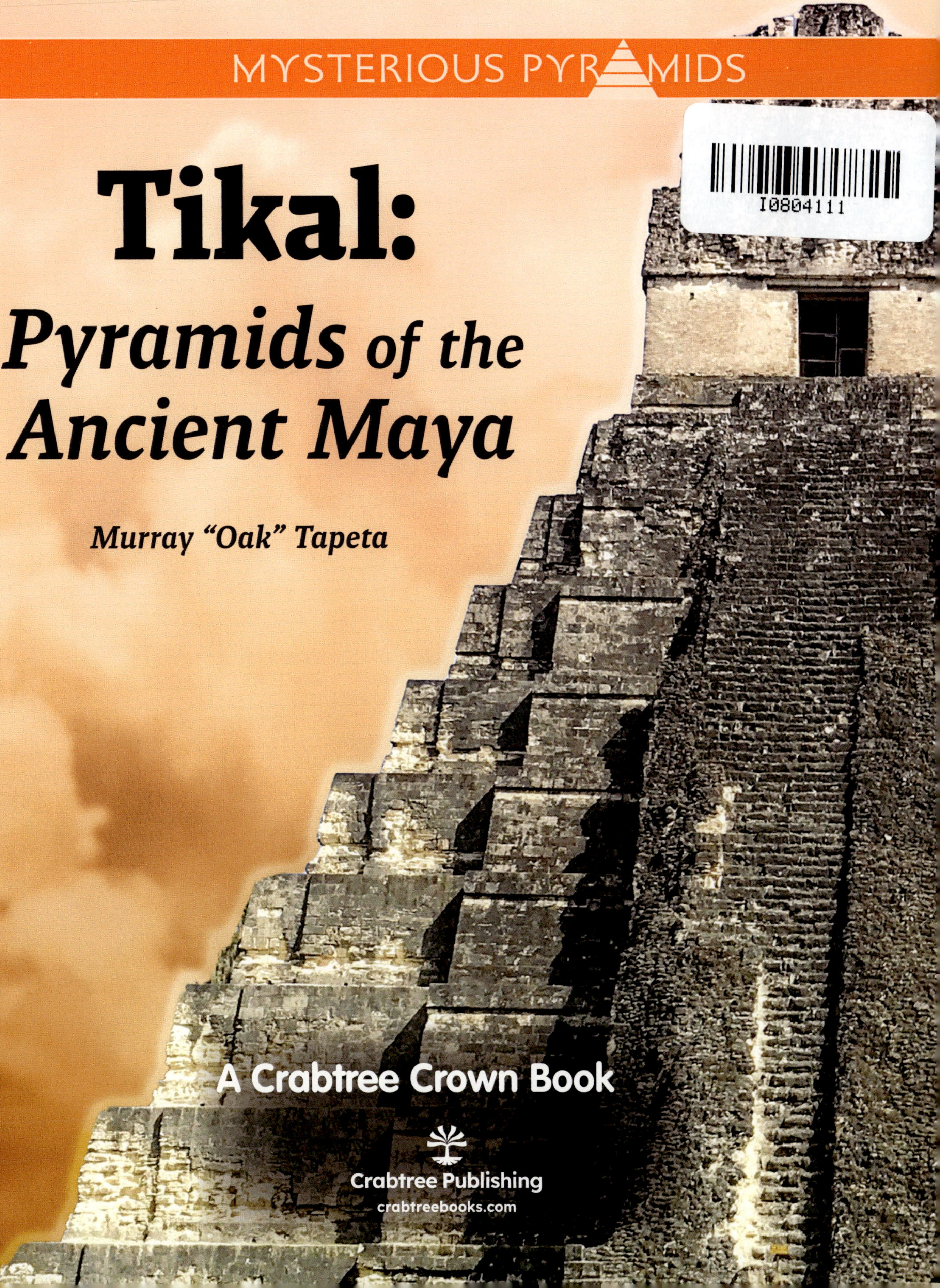

A Crabtree Crown Book

Crabtree Publishing
crabtreebooks.com

Teaching Tips for Caregivers:

You can help your child learn by encouraging them to read widely, both as a leisure activity and as a way of satisfying their curiosity about the world. Reading helps build a strong foundation in language and literacy skills that will help your child succeed in school. This high-interest book will appeal to all readers in intermediate and middle school grades.

Use the following suggestions to help your child grow as a reader.

- Encourage them to read independently at home.
- Encourage them to practice reading aloud.
- Encourage activities that require reading.
- Establish a regular reading time.
- Have your child ask and answer questions about what they read.

Teaching Tips for Teachers:

Engage students throughout the reading process by asking questions like these.

Before Reading

- Ask, "What do you already know about this topic?"
- Ask, "What do you want to learn about this topic?"

During Reading

- Ask, "What is the author trying to teach you?"
- Ask, "How is this like something you have read or seen before?"
- Ask, "How do the text features (headings, index, etc.) help you understand the topic?"

After Reading

- Ask, "In which pyramid did they find the skeleton of Maya ruler Jasaw Chan K'awiil?"
- Ask, "What do you think would have happened if Hernán Cortés had found the Maya city?"
- Ask, "What were the stone tablets called that gave researchers information about the pyramids and past rulers?"

TABLE OF CONTENTS

A PUZZLE FROM THE PAST

The world is full of mysterious places that hold the secrets of lost **civilizations**. Ancient ruins are like snapshots in time. They provide us with important clues about what life was like long, long ago.

Pyramids usually served as grand burial chambers for royalty or as temples for religious ceremonies or both. These structures exist in various forms around the world, built by civilizations that had little or no contact with one another.

The ruins of the ancient Maya city Tikal are preserved in Guatemala's Tikal National Park. **Excavation** of the site revealed a city with a palace at its center, surrounded by six step pyramids.

PYRAMID STYLES

Giza - True pyramid

Maya pyramids are called step pyramids. They have terraces, or flat platforms, on each level and stairways. Each pyramid was dedicated to a god and had a shrine or temple at the top. This was called a **roof comb**.

Teotihuacán - Talud-tablero pyramid

The Maya built their stone cities with materials that were found nearby, such as limestone. **Archaeologists** believe the heavy stones were transported on large wooden rollers and pulled up ramps made of earth with ropes, where builders shaped the limestone with stone and wooden tools.

Ziggurat of Ur - Step pyramid

Borobudur - Step pyramid

2600 BCE
Giza
2500 BCE
2100 BCE
Ziggurat of Ur
2000 BCE
900 BCE
Tikal
259 BCE
Qin Emperor

Tikal - Step pyramid

Qin Emperor - Buried flat-topped, step pyramid

BUILT TO IMPRESS!

Why did so many different ancient cultures build similar towering shapes? Relying on the forces of nature, ancient builders learned that the taller you build, the bigger you had to make the base. This helped distribute the weight more toward the bottom so a very tall structure would not topple over.

210 BCE

100 CE

Teotihuacán

450 CE

778 CE

Borobudur

850 CE

900 CE

MAYA CULTURE

The Maya were a cultural group that developed over thousands of years. At its peak, the Maya civilization reached 2 million people. As many as 100,000 people may have lived in the city of Tikal. The Maya all shared similar customs and lived in hundreds of cities and villages in present-day Guatemala, southern Mexico, Belize, Honduras, and El Salvador.

The ancient Maya built thousands of stone monuments and buildings in the tropical rainforest. Because they were mainly farmers, they studied the positions of stars and planets to determine the best time to plant crops. Among their other achievements, the Maya were beekeepers, creators of a complex calendar and writing system, builders of hundreds of miles of raised roads, and the first people to use cacao seeds to make chocolate.

__Ancestors__ of the Maya still perform rituals and ceremonies at Tikal. Tourists are sometimes allowed to witness ceremonies that celebrate events such as the __equinox__.

WHERE DID THEY GO?

The population began to decrease and the civilization disappeared for unknown reasons around 900 C.E. Theories suggest overpopulation, **depleted** resources, **drought**, or war. But the Maya still exist. DNA shows there are around six million **descendants** living in Mexico and Central America today.

JUNGLE CITY

In the 1500s, European explorers were competing to conquer Central America. In 1525, Spanish **conquistador** Hernán Cortés marched his army through the jungle's giant silk, cedar, cotton, and mahogany trees that grow 130 feet (40 meters) tall.

As Cortés's army made their way through the rainforest, the ruins of the ancient Maya city of Tikal went unnoticed by them. Had they changed their path by 24 miles (39 kilometers), they might have come across the impressive city. Even then, they may have missed the city, long hidden by the overgrown jungle.

Hernán Cortés

Although the ***Indigenous*** *Maya and Aztec people who lived there fought back, they were no match for the invaders' superior weapons.*

A MASSIVE METROPOLIS

Tikal was never truly lost or forgotten. The descendants of the Maya **inherited** their ancient ways. They knew where the ruins of the abandoned city lay, deep in the jungle. Spanish **friars**, led to the remote site by Indigenous guides, wrote about the lost city hidden in the forest. In 1848, the Guatemalan government sent out an **expedition** to determine its exact location.

Teams of archeologists soon followed and began to uncover a vast, ancient city around six square miles (16 square kms) in size. They documented thousands of structures. There were temples, palaces, and public plazas. There were residences, roads, and ball-game courts. Near the city's center stood a prominent palace and six towering pyramids.

Preservation of these structures began in the 1950s. Today archaeologists use aerial laser technology called lidar to "see" beneath the jungle to explore cities.

GIFTS TO THE GODS

Archaeologists tested traces of blood they found on black glass arrowheads and in bowls. They suspected the Maya used them to make blood sacrifices to their gods. They found both animal and human blood on the deadly weapons.

This figure is called a Chacmool, which means "large red jaguar." A Chacmool is a carving of a person carrying offerings to the gods on a plate resting on its stomach.

This painted mural in the Mexican city of Palenque shows a Maya king.

WRITTEN IN STONE

How did researchers learn about the history of the Maya and their city? **Hieroglyphics** carved on **stelae** discovered at the site provided information about the six pyramids. Stelae are four-sided stone monuments that show pictures and writing that mark important events such as the births and deaths of kings and victories in battle. Paintings often depicted everyday life in the ancient city revealing much about their way of life.

Stelae were permanent records made in stone by the Maya. They also recorded their history, religion, and culture on bark in folding books called codices. Only four of these codices survived.

SECRET NAME

Writing on a stela revealed Tikal's true name was Yax Mutal. It was named to honor the ancient ruler Yax Ehb Xook, who founded Tikal's most powerful ruling dynasty around 90 CE.

THE TEMPLE OF THE GREAT JAGUAR

Researchers assigned numbers to the pyramids to help identify them. Temple I is called the Temple of the Great Jaguar. At 154 feet (47m) tall, it has a large roof comb and a **lintel** carved with an image of a king sitting on a jaguar throne. The structure was built around 730 CE.

Carving of ruler Jasaw Chan K'awiil

Inside, they found the skeleton of the Maya ruler Jasaw Chan K'awiil. Also known as Sky Rain, his tomb was excavated by archaeologists in 1958. Around his neck was a necklace made from 114 jade beads. It weighed nearly nine pounds (four kilograms). The temple was constructed around Sky Rain's tomb.

Temple I
Temple of the Great Jaguar

The city's rulers had many names. Jasaw Chan K'awiil was also known as Ah Cacao, which means "Lord Chocolate."

The remains of jaguar skins were found near Sky Rain's body. The tomb contained objects made from precious materials. They included **alabaster**, **jade**, **spondylus** shells, and pearls from the Caribbean Sea. There were also ceramic vessels, plaques, stingray spines, and carved human bones.

Sky Rain's **heir** was his son Yik-in Chan K'awiil. He was called Sun Sky Rain. He finished construction of the second pyramid, Temple II. Also called the Temple of the Masks, it was built to honor his mother, Lady Kalajuun Une' Mo', whose name means Twelve Macaw Tails. Two giant masks of noble women decorated the upper platform.

The Temple of the Great Jaguar appears on the 50 centavos note used in Guatemala.

Temple II
Temple of the Masks

THE TEMPLE OF THE TWO-HEADED SERPENT

The fourth pyramid, Temple IV, was built around 741 CE to honor Sun Sky Rain and show the strength of Tikal. It is called the Temple of the Two-Headed Serpent. Giant wooden lintels inside the temple were carved to show Sun Sky Rain seated beneath a giant snake.

Standing at 212 feet (65 meters), the pyramid is the tallest in Tikal and one of the largest structures built by Indigenous people in the Americas. It is not yet known whether the ruler is buried inside.

Some parts of Maya pyramids were made from sapodilla trees. Wood from these tropical trees has a deep red color and is very hard and dense.

Temple IV
Temple of the Two-headed Serpent

TEMPLE OF THE INSCRIPTIONS

Temple VI also honors Sun Sky Rain. The pyramid was completed around 766 CE and is known as the Temple of the Inscriptions. The back and sides of its roof comb are covered with hieroglyphics. They include a list of dates and events from Tikal's past.

Carving on stelae

Maya alphabet

Temple VI
Temple of the Inscriptions

MYSTERIES IN STONE

At 187 feet (57 meters), the fifth pyramid is the second-tallest in Tikal. Temple V has a single tiny room at the top. Its steep roof comb was once decorated with colorful paintings that could be seen over the treetops. No one knows exactly when or why it was built. It may have been completed around 700 CE.

The third pyramid, Temple III, is called the Temple of the Jaguar Prophet. Archaeologists think it was completed around 810 CE. This was the last pyramid built in Tikal. The mysterious ruler called Dark Sun may be buried inside.

There are other pyramids found in Tikal besides the six main temples. One known as Temple 33 was dismantled by archaeologists in the 1960s. Many people think they were wrong to destroy the structure while looking for clues and treasures.

THE END OF TIKAL

No one knows for sure why the great city of Tikal was deserted. Archaeologists have some theories. Unlike most large cities, Tikal had no rivers close by or other sources of fresh water. Drought may have driven people away. Diseases may have played a part. Nearby farms and forests might not have been enough to support the large population. In its final decades, Tikal was almost always at war with neighboring cities.

By the 10th century, the city was nearly empty. Rainforest plants overtook its grand plazas and palaces. For hundreds of years, Tikal would remain hidden in the dense jungle.

All six of Tikal's great pyramids were built over a period of approximately 100 years, throughout the 700s.

TIKAL TODAY

You can visit Tikal National Park and see the impressive pyramids for yourself. Some can be climbed to take in the magnificent view of the Guatemalan rainforest. Tourists can walk through the once-great city, following in the footsteps of the ancient Maya.

Scientists have been excavating the ruins of Tikal for over 70 years. But the site is so massive that only about 15 percent of it has been uncovered. The work is done slowly and carefully. No one wants to damage irreplaceable structures and **artifacts**. Researchers continue to discover clues that help tell the story of the once mighty city and its pyramids, abandoned in the jungle long ago.

CURIOUS FACT

The Tikal ruins were used to represent the planet Yavin 4 in Star Wars: A New Hope. *In the movie, pyramids can be seen poking up through the lush trees.*

GLOSSARY

alabaster (AL-uh-bas-ter) A smooth, soft, often white stone used for carving

ancestor (AN-sess-tuhr) A person who lived long before someone in the same biological line

archaeologists (ahr-kee-AH-luh-juhsts) Scientists who study the distant past by digging up things that people made, used, and left behind

artifacts (AHR-tuh-fakts) Objects made and used by humans in the past, including tools and weapons

civilizations (siv-uh-li-ZAY-shuhnz) Groups of people with their own language and way of life

conquistador (kahn-KEE-stuh-dor) A person from Spain who sought to conquer the New World, find treasure there, and convert its people to Christianity; Spanish for conqueror

depleted (dih-PLEET-id) Something that has been used up

descendant (dih-SEN-duhnt) A person who is born after someone in the same biological line

drought (drout) A long period without rain or precipitation

equinox (EE-kwuh-noks) One of two times a year where the day and night are both 12 hours long

excavation (eks-kuh-VAY-shun) The process of digging in the soil

expedition (ek-spuh-DISH-uhn) A journey taken for a specific purpose, often for exploration

friar (FRY-er) A member of the Catholic Church who has dedicated their life to poverty and obedience

heir (air) Someone who receives a person's money, property, or title when that person dies, especially the successor to a throne or royal title

hieroglyphics (hire-uh-GLIF-iks) Writing made up of pictures and symbols that stand for words

Indigenous (in-DIJ-uh-nuhs) Referring to the original inhabitants of a particular place

jade (JAYD) A hard, valuable gemstone, often green in color, used for jewelry and ornaments

lintel (LIN-tuhl) A piece of wood, stone, or other material that is placed above a doorway or other opening to support the weight above it

roof comb (roof kohm): A wall rising from the center line of a roof to give an appearance of greater height

spondylus (SPON-duh-luhs) Referring to a mollusk with a thick, colorful shell containing long spines or thorns, also called thorny or spiny oysters

stelae (STEE-lee): Carved stone monuments that show pictures and writing, often on all four sides

INDEX

QUESTIONS AFTER READING

1. Most Maya pyramids are_____.
   a. step
   b. smooth
   c. underground
2. The pyramids at Tikal were built by ______ people.
   a. Aztec
   b. Spanish
   c. Maya
3. Many hieroglyphics at Tikal are found on ______.
   a. trees
   b. stelae
   c. ball courts
4. The pyramid known as Temple 1 is also called _______.
   a. The Temple of the Great Jaguar
   b. The Temple of the Two-Headed Serpent
   c. The Temple of the Inscriptions
5. The six great pyramids at Tikal were mostly built in the ______.
   a. 5th century
   b. 10th century
   c. 8th century

Answers: 1. a, 2. c, 3. b, 4. a, 5. c

ABOUT THE AUTHOR

Murray "Oak" Tapeta was born in a toilet-less cabin in Montana. Growing up in the great outdoors, he learned to love trees. He got the nickname "Oak" after climbing to the top of an oak tree when he was only three years old. Oak loves to read and write. He has written a number of books about fascinating, terrible, and gruesome events from the distant past. He prefers spending time in the wilderness with his dog, Birchy.

Author: Murray "Oak" Tapeta

Editor: Kathy Middleton

Proofreader: Crystal Sikkens

Design: Samara Parent and Kathy Walsh

Production coordinator: Candice Campbell

IMAGE CREDITS

Shutterstock: ©Mohammed_Al_Ali, p 6 (bottom left); ©Aleksandar Todorovic, p 8-9; ©SL-Photography, p 13, 14; ©mure3496, p 15; ©Donnebryant, p 16, 18-19; © meunierd, p 22 (top); ©Rob Crandall, p 28-29

All other images from Shutterstock

Crabtree Publishing

crabtreebooks.com 800-387-7650

In Canada: We acknowledge the financial support of the Government of Canada through the Canada Book Fund for our publishing activities.

Hardcover 978-1-0398-7284-4
Paperback 978-1-0398-7342-1
Ebook (pdf) 978-1-0398-7397-1
Epub 978-1-0398-7446-6

Published in Canada
Crabtree Publishing
616 Welland Avenue
St. Catharines, Ontario
L2M 5V6

Published in the United States
Crabtree Publishing
347 Fifth Avenue
Suite 1402-145
New York, New York, 10016

Library and Archives Canada Cataloguing in Publication
Available at Library and Archives Canada

Library of Congress Cataloging-in-Publication Data
Available at the Library of Congress

Printed in the U.S.A./CP052026